Cheeks on Fire

Raymond Radiguet

Translated from the French by Alan Stone

ALMA CLASSICS

ALMA CLASSICS LTD
London House
243-253 Lower Mortlake Road
Richmond
Surrey TW9 2LL
United Kingdom
www.almaclassics.com

Les Joues en feu first published in French by Bernard Grasset in 1925
This translation first published by John Calder (Publishers) in 1976
This new edition first published by Alma Classics Ltd in 2012

Translation © Alma Classics Ltd
Cover image © Jessica Connett

Printed in Great Britain

Typeset by Tetragon

ISBN: 978-0-71454-373-4

Contents

Foreword

I am publishing these poems in chronological order. It is the only arrangement that befits them as, far from prizing the sort of blind man's buff that some writers play with their readers, I have no wish other than to be understood. On rereading these poems, detached from myself, it seems to me that they can throw some light on an obscure age – the age proper to ingratitude: sixteen, seventeen and eighteen years old. At that time of life, months have the value of years. This last consideration prompted me to let the poems be read as they are written. I preferred to sacrifice typographical amenities rather than extinguish the glow that belongs both to the natural fires of dawn and to less foreseeable fires.

The first of these poems, 'The Language of the Flowers or the Stars', was composed in March 1919, the last of them in August 1921. It was at the time of the latter that I started to write *The Devil in the Flesh*. Since then I have written no more poetry. But if the poem that closes this volume happens to be called 'A Lifeless Swan', no secret intent on my part must be read into this fact.

My fondness for clarity is too strong to keep silent about the mysteries concealed in these poems, or to pretend to be unaware of their existence. These mysteries in no way emerge from an aesthetic, nor are they the result of some wager. I shall never find a justification for them where one would ordinarily look, and why should I authorize an obscurity cultivated by some of my predecessors? If I am to be blamed or praised, no one but me deserves the praise or blame. My poems are the natural expression of a blend of reticence and a hiddenness proper to the age at which they were written. If everything is not clear, there is no point in accusing my favourite poets. Because it is Ronsard, Chénier, Malherbe, La Fontaine, Tristan L'Hermite who taught me what poetry is. Whenever I have dipped into the works of more recent poets, I have been unable to draw any lesson from them, and there is not even one that I would like to imitate. Some wretched masters have taught a whole generation of youth that to get to the heart of things one must strip poems of all their trappings, and that in removing the obstacles one gets closer to the poetry.

Is it an uncommon modesty that makes a poet confess that the most certain interest in his work is doubtlessly psychological in nature? *Cheeks on Fire* might throw light on a mysterious moment: the Birth of Venus, which must not be confused with the Birth of Love. It is before or after the heart that our senses awaken, never at the same time. In addition, these poems do not seem frivolous to me after writing *The Devil in the Flesh*, that drama of the fore-season of the heart. Old men will perhaps reproach me, as they have done before, for lacking youth. One would astound their romantic notions by telling them that they only depreciate and misrepresent things in wishing them to be other than they are, even when they wish them to be more beautiful. Perhaps they will accuse me of libertinism. The optical error that makes people judge a work as licentious when everything is told purely and simply earned my first novel many readers. I hope they were disappointed. But should one even inquire?

Daphnis and Chloé, the most chaste novel in the world, is it not one of the books that schoolboys read in secret? And more men than one would believe remain schoolboys all their lives. Prurient curiosity and schoolboy sniggers! How many people have been able to dispense with them with the years?

Among other things that may mislead the attentive reader, I would like to prevent at least one from doing so. After he has read the first half of this collection and understood that the author intends for each poem a particular shape, he will be surprised to see me adopt a form, no doubt elastic enough in its monotony, but at least, at a glance, quite repetitious. It is because all these octosyllabic poems, rhymed when they sang to me, derive from the same source of inspiration. They were written in March and April 1921, on the shores of the Mediterranean. On its ancient shores, to this naive inhabitant of the Île-de-France, mythology showed itself living and naked. After the nymphs of the Marne, seeing Venus in her bath is enough to turn your head. It is in some of these poems that the most greedy sensuality is least hidden. Then we see the singular apparition of Venus gently disappearing.

– Raymond Radiguet

Cheeks on Fire

Le Langage des fleurs ou des étoiles

J'ai demeuré pendant quelque temps dans une maison où les douze jeunes filles ressemblaient aux mois de l'année. Je pouvais danser avec elles, mais je n'avais que ce droit ; il m'était même défendu de parler. Un jour de pluie, pour me venger, j'offris à chacune des fleurs rapportées de voyage. Il y en eut qui comprirent. Après leur mort, je me déguisai en bandit pour faire peur aux autres. Elles faisaient exprès de ne pas s'en apercevoir. En été tout le monde allait prendre l'air. Nous comptions les étoiles, chacun de notre côté. Lorsque j'en trouvai une en trop, je n'ai rien dit.

Les jours de pluie seraient-ils passés ? Le ciel se referme. Vous n'avez pas l'oreille assez fine.

The Language of the Flowers or the Stars

I stayed for a while in a house together with twelve young girls, each of whom resembled a month of the year. I could dance with them, but that was my only privilege; even the right to talk was refused me. One rainy day, to take my revenge, I presented each of them with flowers brought back from far-off lands. To a few of them, my motive was plain. After they died, I dressed up as a bandit to intimidate the others. They deliberately ignored my costume. When summer came, we all went for walks outdoors. We'd count the stars, each of us using his own method. When I counted one too many, I kept silent.

Should the rainy season have ended by now? The sky draws shut once more. Your ears aren't so finely attuned.

Incognito

Soi-disant diseuse de bonne aventure
On est presque nu
Des portraits de famille
Il y en a qui seraient honteux
Une rue déserte
Plus tard elle portera votre nom
Les nuages descendent à terre
Ils gênent nos pas
Les hommes qu'on a mis en prison
ne se doutent de rien
Des bêtes féroces gardent la capitale
Pourtant nous ne sommes pas bien méchants
La clef des champs
Je vous en prie

Incognito

Would-be fortune-teller
                    We're almost nude
Family pictures
Some might blush
                    A deserted alley
Later she'll take your name
Clouds touch the ground
They get in your way
            Men locked behind bars
            hardly suspect
Wild beasts patrol the capital
Yet we're not so wicked
                        The key to the fields
                        I beg of you

Un soir d'août

L'avenir,
Ici
La dame le prévoit,
Exception faite
Des jours de fête,
Quand on traverse le viaduc.

Les demoiselles d'honneur,
Cela va sans dire,
Se laissent conduire.

De quoi vous plaignez-vous ?
Est-ce ma faute
Si ces rameurs
N'y vont pas de main morte.

Dans les verres
Tiédit l'orangeade.

Un soir d'août,
N'importe lequel.

An Evening in August

The future,
Now
The lady's made provisions
Except for
Feast days,
When they cross the viaduct.

The maids of honour,
Without a doubt,
Are glad to be taken out.

Why all the grumbling?
I'm not to blame
If the oarsmen
Row with lame hands.

In the glasses
The orangeade begins to fade.

An evening in August,
No matter which.

Tombola

On dirait la Grande Roue.

Une broche à l'heureux gagnant ; le pauvre marin, ne sachant qu'en faire, de rage pique au vif l'azur de son béret, et, à défaut d'un prénom de femme, y fait inscrire celui de son bateau.

« Où puis-je avoir laissé mon éventail ? »

« Vous ne voyez pas d'ici ? Il fait la roue, sur la pelouse, où des trèfles à quatre feuilles poussent en cachette. »

Les jeunes filles qui montent en balançoire rougissent chacune à leur tour : leurs robes blanches s'accrochent aux bras de l'épouvantail.

« Elles aussi sont toutes rouges, les cerises. »

Sans faire de jalouses, le galant épouvantail offre des boucles d'oreilles.

Le pauvre marin ne possède d'autre bijou qu'un broche, gagnée à la tombola.

Tombola

So it's the wheel of fortune.

A brooch to the lucky winner; the wretched sailor, having no use for it, wounds the heart of his blue cap, and since no girl-friend comes to mind, he pricks in the name of his ship instead.

"Now where could I have left my fan?"

"Don't you see it? It's strutting about on the lawn, where four-leaf clover secretly flourish."

The girls climbing on the swings turn crimson as, one by one, their white frocks get caught on the scarecrow's arms.

"Cherries are also red from head to toe."

Without playing favourites, the gallant scarecrow hands out a pair of earrings.

The only piece of jewellery that the poor sailor owns is the brooch he won in the lottery game.

Déjeuner de soleil

Ah ! les cornes : c'est un colimaçon.
Paresseuse, si vous voulez nous plaire,
Désormais sachez mieux votre leçon.

Nous ne sommes plus ces mauvais garçons
Ivres à jamais de boissons polaires,
Depuis que les flots vivent sans glaçons.

Seize ans : les glaces sont à la framboise.
Je ne viderai pas votre panier
Avant la mort de cette aube narquoise.

À mon âge les pleurs manquent de charme ;
J'irai près du soleil, dans le grenier,
Afin que sèchent plus vite mes larmes.

Time Will Fade It

Oh, the horns – so it's a snail.
Sluggard, if you wish to please us
Study harder, and you won't fail!

We aren't those same rowdy drunks
Swilling polar concoctions
Since the ice floes have lately shrunk.

Aged sixteen: the ice is raspberry;
I won't ransack your basket
Till the jeering dawn is fit to bury.

At my age, it looks dumb to cry;
I'll climb near the sun, up in the attic,
So that my tears will quickly dry.

Une carte postale : les quais de Paris

On a remplacé les coquillages
Par des boîtes à livres. J'appris
Qu'il est de bien plus jolis rivages,
En feuilletant les livres de prix.

Cher ami, sans retard levons l'ancre ;
Encrier triste comme la mer.
De grâce, n'écrivez plus à l'encre :
Les mots qu'on y pêche sont amers.

A Postcard: on the Banks of the Seine

Stalls of dusty books now take
The place of pretty shells, and thanks
To skimming spicy paperbacks
I know that there are fairer banks.

Dear, let's weigh anchor now;
Inkwell cloudy as the ocean.
Next time you write, use no ink:
Your fishing-reel pen hooks sad emotion.

Emploi du temps

Mécontents si Dimanche ignore les pensums,
Au lieu de mots anglais mâchons du chewing-gum.
Souriez un peu, aurore à mon gré volage :
Le bonnet d'âne sied à ravir à votre âge.

On a le temps de rougir durant les vacances.
Puis après avoir lu tous les livres de prix,
Bouche en cœur, apprends à chanter faux des romances,
Souriant aux rosiers nains qui n'ont pas fleuri.

Une à une mes chansons mouraient en chemin.
« Le lieu du rendez-vous. » Déteigne une pancarte :
Le moindre de mes soucis, pourvu que demain
Les gratte-ciel jalousent mes châteaux de cartes.

Les doigts engourdis à force de réussites,
(Elle dans l'herbe folle perdant la raison)
Mensonges en fleurs ! Les soirs où vous vous assîtes
Les nouai-je en gerbe avec les brins du gazon ?

Votre regard m'accompagne en train de plaisir.
Plus morte que vive sous le pont qui l'outrage,
La rivière roule des sanglots de plaisir.
À la fin eux seuls compagnons de mes voyages.

Conclusion

Lasse de soulever d'indociles collines
Délaisse sans pleurs les pensums que j'inventais ;
Aurore, adieu ! En lambeaux la robe d'été,
Je me sens assez fort pour regagner les villes.

Daily Routine

Sad that Sunday's free from extra chores,
Let's skip these puzzles and chew gum instead.
Smile for me a little, fickle dawn;
A dunce's cap looks stunning on your head.

Over vacation, there's ample time to blush,
Then after reading all the hottest books
Croon sentimental ballads out of tune
And sneer at dwarfish roses in the bush.

One by one, my songs give way to sighs.
"Lovers' nest" – but now the signpost fades;
That doesn't bother me, so long as skyscrapers
Tomorrow jolt my castles in the skies.

My fingers grow numb from too much solitaire
(Amid the rank weeds sits my raving lass)
Flowering lies! At night when we would stroll
Did I tie them into sprays with blades of grass?

In the midst of ecstasy, I see your face.
A stream, beneath the bridge which straddles it,
though violated, heaves with sobs of rapture;
In the end those sobs are all I can embrace.

Sign-off

Weary from trying to bolster flagging hills,
Set aside the chores that I contrived;
Dawn, farewell! Summer's dress all torn,
I think I'm ready to venture back to town.

Paul et Virginie

Ciel ! les colonies.

Dénicheur de nids,
Un oiseau sans ailes.
Que fait Paul sans elle ?
Où est Virginie ?

Elle rajeunit.

Ciel des colonies,
Paul et Virginie :
Pour lui et pour elle,
C'était une ombrelle.

Paul and Virginia

Ye gods! These settlements…

Pillager of nests,
A bird with wings of air.
What does Paul do alone?
And where's Virginia, where?

Growing young and fair.

'Mid settlements in heaven
Virginia wed to Paul:
For both of them it's even
A summer parasol.

Amélie

Vagues charmeuses, ô peut-être votre essaim
Mouille le ramage des vieux oiseaux moqueurs.
Ils se moquent de nous qui perdîmes un cœur,
Cœur d'or que l'océan veut garder en son sein.

Faire entendre raison à des âmes pareilles !
En vain vous gazouillez, bijoux, à ses oreilles.
Cher René nous savons que c'est pure folie,
Ce voyage au long cours à cause d'Amélie.

Amélie

Bewitching waves, perhaps your tossing crests
Waken the mockingbird's jeering cries;
They jeer at us for having lost a prize,
A heart of gold the ocean takes to her breast.

What folly to try to reason with souls like these!
Mockers, deaf ears repel your taunts with ease.
We both agree, René, you're mad to take
This ocean voyage all for Amélie's sake.

Lettres d'un alphabet

Bateau

Bateau debout, bateau hagard,
La danseuse sans crier gare,
Sans même appeler les pompiers,
Mourut sur la pointe des pieds.

Filet à papillons

« Papillon, tu es inhumain !
Je te poursuis depuis hier. »
Ainsi parlait une écolière
Que j'ai rencontrée en chemin.

Hirondelle

Comme chacun sait, l'hirondelle
Annonce la belle saison.
Elle n'a pas toujours raison ;
Cependant nous croyons en elle.

Initiales

Initiales enlacées
Sur le sable comme nous-mêmes :
Nos amours seront effacées
Avant ce fugitif emblème.

Loup

Neige un carnaval insolent ;
Je vous reconnais joli masque :
Ce loup fuyait sous la bourrasque
Des confettis roses et blancs.

Letters of an Alphabet

Ship

Haggard ship, upended ship,
A dancer falling gracefully,
Not even hailing firemen,
Sank (on tiptoe) in the sea.

Butterfly Net

"Butterfly, you're such a brute!
I've followed you since yesterday!"
Were the words of a pouting schoolgirl
Whom I overheard while on my way.

Swallow

As everyone knows, the swallow's song
Tells us that summertime is here.
Though, often as not, the songster's wrong,
We still regard him as a seer.

Initials

Our initials interlaced
In the sand, our bodies too:
Sooner than this memento
Will our love be erased.

Wolf

A carnival of snowflakes eddy;
I recognize your pretty mask:
A wolf that flew, not one to bask
In swirls of pink and white confetti.

Mouchoir

Amiral, ne crois pas déchoir
En agitant ton vieux mouchoir :
C'est la coutume de chasser
Ainsi les mouches du passé.

Tirelire

Enfant bientôt tu sauras lire,
Nous te comblerons de cadeaux.
Une pesante tirelire
Sera ton plus léger fardeau.

Vitre

Voici la mauvaise saison :
Le froid, qui est un assassin,
S'amuse à faire des dessins
Sur les vitres de sa prison.

Handkerchief

Old Admiral, it's no disgrace
To wave your tear-stained handkerchief:
It's common practice thus to chase
Buzzing flies which brought us grief.

Money Box

O child, you soon will learn to read
And then we'll bring you gifts untold.
A filled-to-bursting money box
Will be your very lightest load.

Window Pane

This is the wretched season:
The cold, brute assassin,
Just for fun draws sketches
On the windows of its prison.

Halte

Cycliste en jupe-culotte !

À travers tous les âges, la route nationale mollement se déroule, comme ta bande molletière. Le culte des obstacles est en honneur chez nos ancêtres gaulois : poursuis le petit bonhomme des chemins, malgré la borne kilométrique qui t'invite à la fatigue, au repos de l'amour.

Pause

Cyclist in your culottes!

Throughout the ages, the main road has always lazily unwound like the puttees coiled around your legs. A fetish for obstacles was highly esteemed by your Gallic forefathers: cruise along, ignoring the milestone which recalls you to your weariness and love's respite.

Tombeau de Vénus

Jouets des vagues, vos oreilles roses. Ô mes cousines, plus légères que l'onde, pourquoi l'orphéon océanique vous fait-il frissonner ? Voici Vénus. (Mais si vous voulez grandir, mes petites cousines, vous n'avez pas de temps à perdre.) Aujourd'hui, cueillette des plumes d'autruche ; bouquet de vagues frisées, l'éventail de Vénus.

Si elle se noie, nous lui élèverons un tombeau en coquillages.

The Tomb of Venus

Sport of the waves, your rosy ears. O my cousins, lighter than any wave, why does the booming ocean choir set you quivering? Here's Venus. (But if you want to grow, my little ones, there's no time to lose.) This very day, the gathering of ostrich feathers; tuft of curled waves, the fan of Venus.

If she should drown, we'll build her a tomb out of seashells.

Déplacements et villégiatures

I

Au sein des villes qui ont dès longtemps atteint l'âge de la stérilité, ah si l'encre pouvait se tarir ! Dans un magasin où je cueillais des giroflées de Suède, nous frôlâmes Gertrude que l'on voit une seule fois pendant son séjour sur la terre ou la mer. Enseigne des gantiers : une attrayante image de la mort. Cette main de fer au-dessus de ma tête, n'est-ce pas aussi ma main que ne savent éviter les mouches ?

II

En robe du soir, l'infante de la dune frileuse m'offre son lait. Elle m'apprend à marcher sur le sable sans y laisser de traces. Nous nous exprimons dans des langues plus ou moins mortes. Cependant, le cavalier, à qui la mer va comme un gant, le futur noyé, l'oreille contre les vagues, les écoute décider de son sort, sans comprendre.

Town and Country

I

O, if only the ink would run dry in the bosom of towns which long ago went sterile! In a flower shop where I was picking out pink clover, we brushed past Gertrude who can be glimpsed only once during her sojourn on land or sea. The glove-maker's signboard: a beguiling image of death. That iron hand poised above my head, is it not also my own hand that flies can't evade?

II

In her evening gown, the infanta of the wintry dunes proffers me her milk. She teaches me how to walk on the sand without leaving footprints behind. We talk in mostly dead tongues. Meanwhile, the cavalier – whom the ocean fits like a glove, his future drowned, his ears pressed to the waves – hears them settle upon his fate but fails to grasp their meaning.

Automne

Tu le sais, inimitable fraise des bois
Comme un charbon ardent aux doigts de qui te cueille :
    Leçons et rires buissonniers
    Ne se commandent pas.

    Chez le chasseur qui la met en joue
L'automne pense-t-elle susciter l'émoi
Que nous mettent au cœur les plus jeunes mois ?

    Blessée à mort, Nature,
    Et feignant encor
    D'une Ève enfantine la joue
Que fardent non la pudeur mais les confitures,
      Ta mûre témérité
      S'efforce de mériter
      La feuille de vigne vierge.

Autumn

Matchless wild strawberry, you know full well
(Fingers of live embers having seared your face)
    A teacher's frown and truant's grimace
    Cannot both in one season dwell.

    Is Autumn hoping to assuage
The hunter taking aim at him
With the balm of summer's carefree days?

        Nature, mortally wounded,
        Yet doing all you can to seem
    Like a girlish Eve with blushing cheek
(Jam, not modesty, making their sheen)
         – You rashly cling to the belief
         That you're still mellow enough to wear
         The Virginia creeper's ruddy leaf.

Bouquet de Flammes...

Bouquet de flammes (que délie
Des faveurs l'innocent larcin)
Où se noyer en compagnie
Des colombes de la Saint-Jean.

De l'eau qui ne peut en son lit
Obtenir la tranquillité,
Et des feux oisifs qui s'ennuient
Loin des lieux par Vénus hantés,

Roucoulent les vagues, singeant
Dans leur adorable colère
Un sein qui se gonfle de lait.
Ou de désir ? Plutôt cela.

Bouquet of Flames...

Bouquet of flames (which stolen
Kisses make more bright)
How grand, on Midsummer Day
To drown, with the doves, in your light.

Streams which toss in their beds,
Murmuring ceaselessly,
And restless fires that fume
Far from where Venus treads,

Coo to the waves, and mime
In their adorable fit,
A breast grown full with milk.
Or with desire? That's it.

L'École du soir

Aurore, à nul des cœurs qui saignent,
Ne vas recommander l'école
Où buissonnière on nous enseigne
La douleur plutôt que les jeux.

Un jour, en mousse se déguise
L'espiègle Vénus, et son col
Marin fait le ciel orageux ;
Demain en maîtresse d'école,

Mais marine, non buissonnière.
Ses leçons sont plus à ma guise,
Ignorante, elle qui serait
De ses élèves la dernière !

Vénus charmant les tableaux noirs :
Figure tracée à la craie,
Enfin Vénus s'effacerait,
Ligne à ligne, de nos mémoires.

Evening Classes

Aurora, let no bleeding hearts
Enter your truants' classroom where
Instead of carefree games we learn
Many a lesson in despair.

Mischievous Venus one fine day
Dresses up in ocean foam;
Her frothy limbs stir heaven's fire.
Tomorrow she'll preside as mistress

Over her school in the briny deep.
I much prefer her lessons and
I pity the unresponsive lass
Who comes in last in Venus' class!

Venus charms the blackboards where
The chalk depicts her form so fine,
Till at last, her lesson over,
She fades from memory line by line.

Le Rendez-vous solitaire

Emprunte aux oiseaux leur auberge
Au feuillage d'ardoise tendre !
Loin des fatigues, ma cycliste,
Qui t'épanouis sur nos berges,
Future fleur comme Narcisse,

Tu sembles toi-même t'attendre.
Mais pour que nul gêneur ne vienne,
Je nomme la Marne gardienne,
Ô peu chaste, de tes appâts.
La Marne fera les cent pas.

Si son eau douce va semblant
Plus douce et plus chaste que d'autres,
Ses désirs pourtant sont les nôtres :
Voir bouillir à l'heure du thé
Que l'on prend en pantalon blanc,

Au soleil, ta virginité.

Secluded Meeting

Frequent the tavern of the birds
And make the fluttering leaves your roof!
My cyclist, free from weary toil,
Blossoming on the riverbank
(Flower-to-be like vain Narcissus)

By your own fair image stayed.
Lest some intruder spy you
I appoint the Marne as guardian
Of all your charms, O wanton boy;
See, its waters more slowly run.

Although the watchful Marne may seem
More chaste and pure than other streams
Its yearnings are the same as ours:
To watch as your virginity
(At teatime, in white breeches)

Steams in vapour to the sun.

Nymphe émue

De ta tête, ôte ce panier,
Naguère débordant de fraises,
C'est en prendre trop à son aise,
Tant bien que mal, nymphe, élevée.

Car sur les cendres de tes fraises
Les bravos ont fait relever
Le tulle du lit où repose
La source d'hier, qui se tut.

Nymphe, m'apprivoisent tes cuisses,
Tes jambes à mon cou, statue ;
Je courrais comme ondes bondissent,
Et arrivant en bas se tuent.

(Obligé qui voudrait y boire,
Biche, de se mettre à genoux.)

Nymphe pensionnaire des bois
Me conviant à ce goûter,
Pour que commodément je puisse
Tes sauvages fraises brouter,
Demande aux ronces de ces bois
De lever ton tablier noir :

Ardeur de cheminée, à nous
Forestière tu te révèles,
Ton feu je l'allume à genoux
Comme aux sources lorsqu'on y boit.

Affected Nymph

Lifting that basket from your head
(Basket that brimmed with strawberries once)
You're just a bit too nonchalant,
O nymph, who might be more well-bred.

Raking the ashes of strawberries
Has drawn the curtain from the bed
Where the stream of bygone days flowed by
Until it suddenly ran dry.

Nymph whose wild thighs tamed me,
Who clasped me like a statue,
I raced to you like waves that crash
And drown when they reach the bottom.

(All who come to drink, my doe,
On their knees before you first must go.)

Schoolgirlish nymph of the woods
Inviting me in for a snack
So that I might leisurely
Nibble your wild strawberries,
Entreat the brambles of those woods
To lift up your jet-black apron.

The fire crackles once more:
You've proved yourself a real Girl Scout;
Down on my knees I stoke your flame
And drink at the stream where once I came.

Les Adieux du coq

Que le coq agite sa crête
Où l'entendent les girouettes ;
Adieu, maisons aux tuiles rouges,
Il y a des hommes qui bougent.

Âme ni mon corps n'étaient nés
Pour devenir cette momie
Bûche devant la cheminée
Dont la flamme est ma seule amie.

Vénus aurait mieux fait de naître
Sur le monotone bûcher
Devant lequel je suis couché,
La guettant comme à la fenêtre.

Nous ne sommes pas en décembre ;
Je ne serais guère étonné
Pourtant, si dans la cheminée,
Un beau matin je vois descendre

Vénus en pleurs du ciel chassée,
Vénus dans ses petits sabots.
(De Noël les moindres cadeaux
Sont luxueusement chaussés.)

Mais, Écho ! je sais que tu mens.
Par le chemin du ramoneur,
Comme en un miroir déformant,
Divers fantômes du bonheur,

À pas de loup vers moi venus,
Surprirent corps et âmes nus.
– Bonheur, je ne t'ai reconnu
Qu'au bruit que tu fis en partant.

The Rooster's Farewell Song

May the rooster shake its crest while
Spinning weathervanes are giving ear;
Farewell, broad barns with red tiles,
It's time I hoofed it out of here!

Neither my body nor soul was meant
To become a sleepy log and end up
Fuming below a chimney vent
With a dying flame my only friend.

Venus wishes she'd been born
In the fireplace before which I
Am keeping my lifeless body warm,
Waiting for her to saunter by.

Although December isn't here
I'm sure I'd scarcely be amazed
If one fine morning, while I gazed,
Right before me should appear

Venus in tears, from heaven barred,
Venus in her dainty shoes.
(At Christmas time the smallest gifts
Must come with ribbons and a card.)

Echo, you're lying, or something's amiss,
For through the chimney sweep's tunnel,
As if in a funhouse mirror,
Ever-changing phantoms of bliss

Come softly creeping past my chair
As soul and body gasp for air.
– Rapture, I only knew it was you
From the hiss you made as you went up the flue.

Reste étendue, il n'est plus temps,
Car il vole, âme, et toi tu cours,
Et déjà mon oreille avide,
Suspendue au-dessous du vide,

Ne perçoit que la basse-cour.
Coq, dans la gorge le couteau
Du criminel, chantez encor :
Je veux croire qu'il est trop tôt.

Lie back, my soul, one can't avoid
The march of time, or your own flight;
My greedy ear, athirst for sound
And straining at whispers in the void

Hears only the farmyard's rural king.
Rooster, with the knife that kills
Stuck in your throat, hoarsely sing:
I'd like to think it's early still.

Vénus démasquée

Vénus non seulement me livre
Ses secrets, mais ceux de sa mère :
Jadis je regardais la mer
Comme regarderait les livres

Un enfant qui ne sait pas lire.
Vénus, sans l'aide d'une mère,
D'être venue aux cieux déments
Se vante. Il faut souffrir, déesse,

Qu'un simple élève vous démente.
M'apprendre à lire couramment
Les vagues de la mer qui sont
Maternelles rides d'un ventre,

Voilà bien de vos maladresses !
Et celle d'un naïf garçon
Est ma vengeance : pour le prix
De vos dangereuses leçons,

À me lire je vous appris.

Venus Unmasked

Venus not only reveals to me
Her secrets, but those of her mother too:
Long ago, I'd gaze at the sea
The way a child who couldn't read

Might skim through the pages of a book.
Venus boasts a pedigree
From lofty skies, denying the debt
She owes her mother. Goddess, admit

That a teen-aged novice belies your tale.
I'm really not impressed by your boasts
Because you've taught me how to read
The booming waves, those soft maternal

Wrinkles on the ocean womb.
But I'll repay you as befits
An artless youth: since you let me enrol
As a pupil in your risky school,

I'll teach you how to read my soul.

Les Fiancés de treize ans

Avec la pointe du canif
(Il ouvre non moins aisément
La coquille chère aux amants,
Qu'un nom s'imprime en l'arbrisseau,

Où l'amour dans les cœurs naïfs),
Avec la pointe du canif,
Aiderons-nous Vénus à naître ?
L'oursin du désir se hérisse.

À quoi servira ce trousseau,
De Vénus naïve nourrice,
Débordante, écume, de lait
Par toi comme plages ourlé :

Nulle robe ne peut soumettre
Celle qui, puérile nue,
Dans un coquillage vécut,
En attendant le jour de naître.

Rendez-vous au prochain été.
Patience ! La mer nous attend
Tout au bout de cet an scolaire
Les replis de sa vaste ombrelle

Sauront nos amours abriter
De la maternelle colère.
– Mais toi tu nous comprends, Vénus,
Chère folle, toi qui déjeunes

De soleil et de lune dîne.
Mis à l'école des ondines
On nous apprend à rester jeunes,
À nous qui voudrions vieillir !

Fiancés at Age Thirteen

With the point of a penknife
(Which can just as easily slit
The shell that lovers prize, as it
Can carve a name in a tree's bark

Or strike love into pliant hearts)
With a penknife's point, couldn't we
Somehow assist at the birth of Venus?
Sea urchins' spines stand erect.

This hope chest has no other use
But to serve as wet nurse to Venus,
Brimming, O foam, with frothy milk
Like the spray you toss upon the sand.

No gossamer bridal veil can quell
The girlish nude who patiently
Endured her stay inside a shell,
Waiting to leave her ocean womb.

Next summer we shall keep our tryst.
Be patient! The sea awaits us at
The very end of the school year, when
The folds of her scudding parasol

Will do their best to shield our amorous
Frolics from maternal ire.
– But Venus, you understand us, darling
Rascal, you who breakfast on

Bright sunbeams, and on moonbeams sups.
Sent to school where undines go
We learn to love yet never age,
We who tried to act so sage!

À la dînette de la vie,
À peine mis notre couvert,
Peureux d'être découverts
Par la nourrice de son frère

(De sa mère le préféré :
Dernier venu, c'est le premier ;
Aussi bien, tu le sais, Vénus),
Comme oursin peureux se hérisse.

La naïve à qui l'on défend
De mettre un pantalon ouvert.

– Tu vas me trouver bien enfant
Ondine, si je te demande

De me prêter un des canifs
Qui semblent furtives sardines
Ouvrant le fruit des mers gourmandes.
En échange de ton canif

D'argent, ondine, je dédie
À tes sœurs et à toi l'écorce
Dont je ne sus venir à bout
Assis, couché, ou bien debout,
Trahi par mes naïves forces.

At the dolls' tea party that is life
We've scarcely set the table out of
Fear of being caught in the act
By that jealous spy, her brother's nurse

(That brother who is much preferred,
Last in line, yet always first;
Venus, you know wherefore I speak).
Sea urchin's spines go limp and weak.

Pity the child who was forbidden
To wear frilled drawers, or keep them hidden!

Undine, you'll say I'm just a child
If politely I ask you to

Loan me one of those penknives
Which glisten like slippery sardines
Nibbling open the choicest shellfish.
In exchange for the silver blade

Of your knife, undine, I'll try to carve
Words to you and your sisters on
The bark I couldn't penetrate
Before, whether prone or erect,
Crushed by a force I couldn't direct.

L'Étoile de Vénus

Après d'avril la verte douche,
Dans ton hamac, dans ton étoile,
Au milieu du ciel tu te sèches.
Recommence ! d'une fessée,
Insolente, récompensée.

Sous l'étoile des maraîchers,
Leurs tombereaux de grosses roses
Que par gourmandise l'on baise,
Joues jalouses du châtiment
Que, jaillie hors du gant, ma main,
Frais jet d'eau, inflige à leurs sœurs,

Les fruits qui fondent dans la bouche
Avec le sucre du péché,
Les transporte sur nos marchés
Conduit, Vénus, par ton étoile,
En charrette, un de nos rois mages.
Ils ne t'auront pas empêché
De prendre du ciel le chemin.

Pourquoi donc après être né
Faudrait-il, Vénus, que l'on meure ?
Mais de sa dernière demeure
Déesse, au moins, laisse le choix

À ce serviteur que tu choies
Au point de l'admettre en ta couche.

Au fond du ciel, non de la mer,
Prise aux filets que tu tendis,
Si tu veux, ondine de l'air,

The Star of Venus

After a drenching in April shower,
Stretched in your hammock, high in your star,
You dry yourself before our eyes.
It's raining again! Impudent one,
This spanking is your just reward.

Beneath your star the truck-farmers toil,
Their pushcarts laden with pregnant roses
Whose petals invite the ripest kisses,
Red cheeks athirst for chastisement
Which my hand, fresh spurt of water,
With no glove on, bestows on their sisters

The luscious fruit that melts on your tongue
With the ambrosial taste of sin;
Venus, one of the Three Wise Men,
Guiding his cart by your star's light,
Brings these goods to our marketplace.
To those three kings 'twere no disgrace
To gaze on you in your starry height.

Why then, Venus, are we born
Only to fade and slowly die?
Be kind, at least, and let your
Faithful servant choose his last abode,

This servant whom you might allow
To taste the raptures of your bed.

In heaven's depths (not the sea's)
Caught in the net you drew so fine,
Undine of air, if you would have me

Que ton cœur, ton corps, je réchauffe,
Ne me promets ton paradis,
Mais, dans les Méditerranées,
De dormir où Vénus est née.

Ignite your heart, your body too,
Don't promise to send me to heaven's bourne,
But in the Mediterranean blue
Let me sleep where Venus was born.

Statue ou épouvantail

Les seins du marbre, mes fruits lourds
Arrondis par le lourd soleil,
S'ils rougissent, tout est perdu,
Je les nomme pommes d'amour.

C'est, entier, un verger marin,
À elle seule que Vénus;
Verger par lui-même trahi !
Car Vénus, pendant son sommeil,

Nous livre ses secrets, ses fruits.
(Installé le moineau, corail
Sur ta branche, il la fait plier),
Heureux qui ne doute de rien.

Sans crainte, vagues, picotez
L'arbre du corail effronté :
Dans son rôle d'épouvantail
Vénus manque d'autorité.

Statue or Scarecrow

Those marble breasts, my swollen fruit,
Ripened by the sultry sun,
If they turn red, the deed is done
– Hence I christen them apples of love.

This sprawling orchard in the deep
Is the sovereign realm of Venus
And yet she gives away its secrets
For, while lying fast asleep,

She lets us glimpse her precious fruit.
(A sparrow, on your coral arm,
Bends it without the least alarm),
Lucky are those who can blissfully sleep.

Arise, O waves, and prick fine holes
In this brazen coral skeleton:
Posing as a scarecrow, Venus can't
Convince us that she's adamant.

Le Prisonnier des mers

Le mousse mis en quarantaine,
Sa mère des terres lointaines
Lui fait parvenir des albums
Indéchirables, et son cœur
Ne pourrait pas en dire autant.

C'est le décor des scarlatines ;
On s'y promène sans bouger,
Toujours en chemise de nuit,
Aussi longue que les journées.

Au théâtre des scarlatines
Où meurt le prisonnier des mers,
Jamais on ne boit ni ne mange,
C'est l'apprentissage des anges ;

Son apprentissage fini,
Le prisonnier des mers s'évade,
Il grimpe tout en haut du mât.

Mais les marins ont des fusils,
Oiseau de mer, ange lourdaud,
Une âme retombe dans l'eau,

Parmi, vagues, vos blancs soucis
De pigeons avant le voyage.

Moi je tire à la courte paille,
Pour savoir laquelle de vous
S'en ira prévenir la mère.

The Captive of the Seas

The ship's boy put in quarantine,
His mother, from a distant shore,
Sends him tearproof albums, as
Her aching heart could not say more.

The stage-setting for scarlet fever:
Prowling about while fast asleep,
Clad in a shabby nightdress that's
At least as long as the days that creep.

There, in the darkened theatre
Where the sea's prisoner's dying,
Eating and drinking are not in the script
(For this is an angel's apprenticeship);

His apprenticeship over at last,
The sea's captive makes his exit
And clambers up the tallest mast.

But the sailors with guns take aim;
Bird of the sea, awkward angel,
Sinks homeward, whence he came,

Falling, waves, amid your foam
Bristling like pigeons before ships sail.

And I draw lots, so as to know
Which of those pigeons to choose
To bring his mother the sorry news.

Le Panier renversé

(Histoire de France)

La vie est sommeil dont nous tire
La mort, par les pieds, les cheveux.

Exauçant mes timides vœux
Comme c'est gentil à vous, reine,
D'avoir voulu, vous, en personne,
M'entr'ouvrir du parc de Versailles
La porte, avec la clef des songes.

Pour me faire à nouveau plaisir
Roulez-vous sur votre gazon
Dont le peuple jaloux disait
Qu'en même temps que vos moutons
Le coiffeur royal le frisait.

Car des deux maris, le jaloux,
Que s'en aillent vos jeux, vos ris
Vers cette bergère : Versailles,
C'était non le roi, mais Paris.

Semblant dans le gazon chercher
De Gygès la bague perdue
Vous vous promeniez entre amies,
Respirant un peu, en cachette.

Un amant, il l'eût pardonné ;
Mais pareils jeux de pensionnaires
Ne les peut comprendre un mari.

Avouez, Marie-Antoinette,
(Et bien qu'en public je sois prêt

The Overturned Basket

(A Lesson in French History)

Life is a nap from which Death dares
To yank us by our feet and hair.

How kind of you, Queen, to grant my humble
Wish, and with the key of dreams
To unlock the gate to the grounds of Versailles
With your very own Most Royal Hand.

To fill me, Ruler, with delight,
Let me see you roll on the lawn
Which the lying rabble, out of spite,
Said the royal barber sheared
Along with the sheep you dote upon.

You sport two husbands: Paris, one,
Your jealous mate, you coldly shun
Although he's king. You'd rather run
To the bland amusements of Versailles.

Blithely romping in the grass
As if you were searching for Gyges' ring,
You keep your playmates occupied
(Panting a little on the side).

A husband might condone a lover
Yet frown upon his wife's gay whirl
With her merry troupe of clinging girls.

Marie Antoinette, it's time you owned
(And I am ready to retract

À soutenir tout le contraire),
Que ces prétextes de main-chaude,
Les parties de saute-mouton,

Étaient un peu moins innocentes
Que jeux d'agneaux venant de naître.

Un beau jour le mari jaloux,
Pour venir à bout de sa reine
Demande l'aide du docteur.

Elle se morfond et lamente
Dans l'humiliante prison,
Dans cette chemise de nuit
Juste laissant libre la tête.

Vous n'êtes au bout de vos peines,
Marie-Antoinette, sachez
Que ne vous seront inutiles
Aucun des jeux que vous apprîtes.

Puisqu'ils sont bel et bien partis
Les jours des rubans aux paniers,
Passez la tête à la lucarne
Où l'on voit le Prince Charmant.

Et que nulle arrière-pensée
Ne gâche l'ultime partie
De saute-mouton, de main-chaude :
Bientôt votre main sera froide.

Des perles de votre collier
Gygès suivra le pointillé,
Car à ce mince col de cygne
La bague de Gygès suffit

Every word, though it be fact)
That all those games of hide-and-seek
and leapfrog with your girlfriends were

A bit less chaste and innocent
Than you and your lambs would have us believe.

Then one day the jealous mate,
To turn the tables on his queen,
Calls the doctor on the scene.

And now she kicks her heels and broods,
Locked in prison shamefully,
Wearing a threadbare nightgown which
Just barely lets her head turn free.

Marie Antoinette, know full well,
Your troubles have only just begun,
But you'll be able to put to use
all those games you learned so well.

Those days when baskets were finely laced
With ribbons never more shall be,
So peek through the dormer window to see
If sweet Prince Charming draws apace.

And to make sure your final games
Of hide-and-seek and leapfrog
Won't be spoilt by thoughts of your escape:
Soon your hand will be quite lame.

Gyges will cut on the dotted line
Etched by your gleaming rope of pearls,
For with your slender neck so fine
The ring of Gyges should suffice

Pour escamoter votre tête.
Du saute-mouton en public
Clandestines sœurs, vos amours,
En serait-ce le souvenir,

Ou le roulement des tambours
(Trapèze !) au moment du péril
Qui vous fait peur, ô débutante ?

Mais, tressé pour des bergeries
Moins sanglantes, de ce panier
Bien que de rubans défleuri
Vous rassure la vue. À tort.

Plus la peine de vous cacher
Parmi les arbres de Versailles,
Mon bel arbuste foudroyé,
Au bout du plaisir, qui, d'un jet
Peu féminin, jusques au ciel
Lancez oiseau et sève mièvres.

C'est le coup de foudre, dit-on.
Soyez plus farouche, ma reine,
Et pour lucidement goûter
La pomme d'amour que vous offre
La mort, oui le Prince Charmant,
Refusez que l'on vous endorme.

Déjà la vie est long sommeil
Sous les pommiers au bois dormant,
Et ses songes font dire à l'homme
Qu'il ne dort pas. Nous crûmes vivre,
Éternité ! Heureusement
Que de toi la mort nous délivre.

To whisk your head off in a trice.
Will your severed head be token of
The games of leapfrog you used to play,
Your secret sisters, torrid affairs,

Or of the drum's insistent roll
(Heads up!) at the moment of truth when you,
O debutante, were rattling too?

The basket that holds your butchered head
Sports a faded ribbon which
Assures you that you're heading for
Greener pastures in the sky.

Don't think that you can camouflage yourself
Amidst Versailles' tall trees,
My lovely shrub, blighted at last,
For with a ravishing (if scarcely feminine)
Spurt from your neck, you've scared off
Nesting birds with your shooting sap.

They say you simply lost your head;
Be braver, now, my sorry Queen,
And, to fully savour the bittersweet
Apple of love which your suitor Death
(Yes, fair Prince Charming) proffers you,
Don't let yourself be lulled to sleep.

This life we live is a lengthy nap
'Neath apple trees in sleepy woods
Where dreams convince us that we really
Sleep not at all – Eternity,
How lucky that, when life is through,
Death shall deliver us from you.

À *une promeneuse nue*

Prends exemple sur la colline
Qui doit accoucher du raisin.
Elle, des feuilles de ses vignes,
Pourrait aussi se contenter.

Pourtant, des châles en gazon,
De la fourrure des buissons,
Des bonnets, des manchons de thym
Où cachent leurs jeux les lapins,

Elle costume sa beauté.
– Et toi, coquette extravagante,
Qui de ta seule peau te gantes,
Avril, tu te crois en été !

To a Nude Stroller

Be like a grassy hill which,
Giving birth to grapes, feels quite content
To clutch the leaves of a few stray vines
To cover up this rare event.

But no... with blouses spun from grass,
With bushes which for furs might pass,
With muffs and bonnets made from thyme
(Where rabbits mask their sport sublime)

The hill puts on her fancy wear.
– Yet you, O April, naked flirt
(Whose fair skin is her only skirt)
Must think that summer's already here!

La Guerre de Cent Ans

Ô girls comme flammes danseuses !
Une biche lèche une rose ;
Avec douceur, bonbon anglais,
Elle s'écroule en mon palais.

Si nos langues ne sont pas sœurs,
Qu'une biche lèche mon âme,
Le guerrier, sous d'expertes flammes
S'énerve et pourtant vierge meurt.

Que ne suis-je elle ou l'oiseleur,
Belle sous la boule de gui,
Et au miel de votre baiser,
Oiseleur je resterai pris.

De nos bergères les Anglais
Font des bûches pour leur Christmas.
Fond votre langue en mon palais ;
C'est à la mort que ma grimace

S'adresse et non pas à l'amour.
Je n'ai rien de commun, sauf l'âge,
Avec le dédaigneux Narcisse,
Ainsi que Jeanne trop penché

Sur le seul bûcher de son âme.

The Hundred Years War

Chorus girls like prancing flames!
A doe gently licks a rose
Whose petals, luscious sugardrop,
Slowly crumble in my mouth.

If our tongues be not entwined
May that same doe lick my soul;
The soldier, under heavy fire,
Gets cocky but a virgin dies.

Out to nab a flighty bird
I stoop beneath the mistletoe
Where the sticky honey of your kiss
Ensnares poor me, a truant fowler.

The English turn our easy chairs
Into logs for their Yuletide fires.
Let my palate melt your tongue;
It's not love's rapture that inspires

My wry grimace, but the taste of death.
Except for years I'm not like cold
Narcissus, blind to all your charms,
Who, like Saint Joan, had as his goal

The burning stake fixed in his soul.

L'Ange

Au front de bon élève, l'ange
Lauré de fleurs surnaturelles.

Pour ne pas manquer ses calculs,
Appliqué, il tire la langue,
Tentant de suivre à cloche-pied,
Au verger des quatre saisons,
Le pointillé de leurs frontières.

La neige, est-ce bon à manger ?
L'ange pillard en a tant mis
Dans sa poche, à jamais il reste
Parmi nous les forçats terrestres
Que cette boule rive au sol,
Faite en neige qu'on croit légère.

Sans cesse empêché dans son vol,
Comme nous dans notre délire,
Cet ange enchaîné bat des ailes,
De ses amis implorant l'aide ;
Aussitôt qu'il s'élève un peu,
Retombe dans les marronniers,
Où la gomme de leurs bourgeons
S'accrochant à ses cheveux d'ange
L'empêche à jamais de nier.

Croyez-vous que ce soit pour rien,
Qu'au poirier le pépiniériste
Laisse blettir ses belles poires ?
C'est qu'on reconnaît le voleur,
À la molle empreinte du doigt.

The Angel

With the brow of an all-A pupil, the angel
Wreathed in supernatural flowers.

Trying not to botch up his sums
The flustered angel sticks out his tongue
Then lamely makes his way along
The dotted line on the furthest rim
Of the orchard of the four seasons.

Is crystal snow so good to eat?
The looting angel, having stuffed
His pockets with snow, which he fancied light,
Finds that he's so weighted down
He has to remain with us thieves below
Whom frozen snow has stuck to the sun.

Carelessly thwarted in his flight
(Like us in our delirium)
The angel vainly beats his wings,
Entreating friends to help him out;
No sooner does he rise an inch
Than he plummets into a chestnut grove
Where spacious trees with sticky buds
Pin him down by snow-white tresses,
Forever silencing his denial.

You don't suppose the gardeners
Would negligently let their pears
Turn overripe on fruity trees?
– The fingerprints that prowlers leave
On fruit will give them away with ease.

Mais Dieu examine les mains
Des anges voleurs de framboises,
Des assassins, chaque dimanche,
Et dans les mains les plus sanglantes,
Met des livres dorés sur tranches.

Dites ce que sont vos prisons,
Demande l'ange par trop niais,
Aux deux gendarmes l'emmenant
Avec pièce à conviction,
Dans le char des quatre saisons.

But God inspects the soiled hands
Of angels (innocents with clubs
Who loot the choicest raspberry shrubs)
And places in the reddest palms
Finely gilded books of psalms.

"Confess this world is but your prison!"
Our angel, being a bit naive,
Cries to the guards who pack him off,
Along with all his earthly spoils,
Into the cart of the four seasons.

Septentrion, dieu de l'amour

Nous sommes venus voir l'enfant
Qui, de la pauvre Cendrillon
Ayant, paraît-il, hérité,
Peut conduire sans arrêter
Trois jours durant le cotillon.

Le croyez-vous, c'est celui-ci
Qui danse, une étoile à son front,
Comme sur le parquet poli
Où aurait pu glisser Narcisse.
Son étoile en la mer se mire,
Celle qui guide nos marins.

Tous les cadeaux que distribue
Avec sur les yeux un bandeau
L'enfant qui devrait être dieu
Gracieusement aux danseuses
Ravissent leur cœur et leurs yeux.

De mélodieux coquillages
Des danseuses devinant l'âge.

Des jumelles faisant voir nue
Celle dont on rêve la nuit.

Des chapeaux de bizarre forme
Coiffez-vous-en, car ils endorment
Toute peine qui vient du cœur.
Et, sans nulle parcimonie,
Encor des cœurs, beaucoup de cœurs,
Que gauchement elles manient.

Septentrion, God of Love

We have come to see the child
Who, it seems, having learned
A thing or two from Cinderella,
Could dance without a minute's rest
For three whole days at a gala ball.

Would you believe it, he's dancing now,
A gleaming star upon his brow,
Across a polished floor which vain
Narcissus might have deigned to tread.
His star, which the sea reflects, it's one
Which guides our sailors in the night.

This infant, born to be a god,
Graciously bestows on all
The dancers (since he's quite naive)
Scores of marvellous presents which
Entrance their hearts, astound their eyes...

Shells which sing melodious tunes
Whose age the dancers cannot guess,

Binoculars which show them all
The things that fill their dreams at night,

Hats of every size and shape
(Put one on, for they'll relieve
Your heart of all its bitter grief)
And, flowing by in endless streams,
Broken hearts, battered hearts,
Which the awkward dancers bruise some more.

Si notre feu dure trois jours
Est-il digne du nom amour ?
Ma belle danseuse inconnue
Consulte à ce sujet Vénus
Bien qu'elle n'ait pas reconnu
Pour fils le vrai dieu de l'amour.

Comment veux-tu que nous croyions
En celui qui ne meurt jamais ?
Le vrai dieu c'est l'enfant aimé
C'est le danseur Septentrion ;
Avec le bal son cœur s'arrête
Et notre amour meurt aussi vite.

If our flame should live three days
Does it deserve the name of love?
O my lovely unknown dancer,
Let's put this question to Venus, though
She wouldn't acknowledge the true love-god
To be her own resplendent son.

Did you think that we could put much faith
In a love-god who never dies?
The true love-god is that darling boy,
Septentrion, our lavish friend;
When the ball is over, his heartbeat stops,
And then our love must surely end.

Élégie

Araignée. À moins que l'espoir
Du matin dure jusqu'au soir,
La voilette en fils de la vierge
Dérobera notre adultère.

Ariane, faudrait-il taire
Ta chance d'être parvenue
À démêler tous ces mystères
Où s'embrouillait même Vénus,
Y perdant pied, perdant haleine,
Comme nous dans ses tendres pièges.

Êtes-vous pelote de laine,
Mon cœur, par la chatte agacé ?

Vierge, voici le fil cassé.
C'est bien de ta faute, Vénus,
Puisque nos cœurs sont la pâture
De tes tigres en miniature.

Et la Parque pendant ce temps
Tisse des bonnets de coton,
Pour que les anges en pantoufles,
Visitant les vivants qui souffrent
Les coiffent telle une bougie

De l'éteignoir. Fais-tu défaut,
Coiffure de mon élégie,
Sur les âmes eux-mêmes soufflent ;
Mais les anges sont des ténors
Se ménageant pour chanter haut
Notre louange, dès la mort.

Elegy

Spider lady, unless the fires of dawn
Simmer till dusk,
Your gossamer veil
Will cloak our adulterous tryst.

Ariadne, could you hush up about
The luck you had in
Unravelling all these mysteries
Which even tripped up Venus,
Who lost her footing, her breath too,
Like us who're caught in her gentle snares?

Are you a ball of wool, my heart,
Pelted by catlike claws?

Virgin, now the thread is snapped
And it's all your fault, Venus,
Since our hearts are the feeding ground
For your pygmy tigers.

Meanwhile Clotho, spinner of fate,
Weaves bonnets out of cotton
So that angels wearing slippers
Can descend to those who suffer
And cap our heads
Like a snuffer drawn over a flame.

O bonnets of my elegy,
You're of no avail to
Souls who extinguish themselves.
But the angels are tenors,
Conserving their breath to sing in lofty voices
Paeans to us from the moment we die.

Poésie

De son amour noircir les murs,
C'est très difficile à la ville ;
Souvent les murs étant de verre
Aux patineurs je porte envie

Mais me contente de mes vers ;
Seuls les voleurs sont assez riches
Pour inscrire sur la vitrine
Le prénom de leur bien-aimée.

Que ton diamant, Poésie,
Une de ces vitrines raye,
Des bavardes boucles d'oreilles,
J'achète ou vole le silence

Pour en orner de roses lobes.
Patineur, la glace est rompue
(En belle anglaise copiée,
Ma poésie, avec ses pieds).

Poetry

In the city it's difficult
To darken walls with words of love.
Though city walls are as smooth as ice
I envy skaters their scribbling blades

But with my verse I'll rest content.
Only burglars are rich enough
To etch on gleaming window panes
The first names of their fairest jewels.

Poetry, may your hard diamond
Streak some shop window's face;
The noisy earrings I shall buy
(Shattering the glassy silence)

Will whisper words to rosy lobes.
Skater, the ice is broken now
(And copied in a hand so neat,
My lines of verse, on gliding feet).

Avec la mort tu te maries...

Avec la mort tu te maries
Sans le consentement des dieux ;
Mais le suicide est tricherie
Qui nous rend aux joueurs odieux,
De leur ciel nous fermant la porte.

Les morts que l'on n'attendait pas
Devant le ciel font les cent pas
Et leurs âmes sont feuilles mortes
Jouets du vent, des quatre vents.

Parce qu'au ciel on garde l'âge
Que l'on avait en arrivant,
Narcisse se donne la mort ;
Il n'y trouve nul avantage,
Sauf la volupté du remords.

S'il tenait tant à son visage,
Que ne pensa-t-il se noyer
Dans la fontaine de Jouvence ?
Toi, colombe dépareillée,
Explique à quoi cela t'avance
De répéter de ce nigaud
La dernière parole ? Écho,
Entendons-nous sous ce bosquet,
Es-tu colombe ou perroquet ?

De ce dernier tu t'autorises,
Paresseuse, pour grimacer
Aux mots d'amour que ton Narcisse
N'eut pas souci de prononcer.

You Join with Death...

You join with Death in wedlock though
The gods have not approved the match;
But suicide's a paltry trick
Which earns the wrath of other souls
Who firmly shut fair heaven's gate.

Those who soar to heaven unexpectedly
Cannot gain entrance
For their souls are newly fallen leaves,
The captive sport of the four winds.

Narcissus, ravished by the thought
That souls above don't age beyond
Their day of arrival, slew himself;
The only joy he found there was
The giddy rapture of remorse.

If he was so vain as to worship his looks
To the point of death, why didn't he go
And drown himself in the Fountain of Youth?
And you, O dove without a mate,
Kindly tell me what is gained
By mimicking the dying words
Of that idiot? Echo, from your
Grove send forth a reply I merit:
What's your nature – dove or parrot?

Taking your cue from the latter bird,
Lazy mime, you hoarsely croak
The words of love which your Narcissus
Mumbled in his distractedness.

Lui, Narcisse, errant dans les vals
De la mort, et, de roche en roche,
Elle dans la vie, ils se valent.
Ce désœuvrement les rapproche ;
Qu'ils eussent fait un beau ménage !

Narcissus, wandering in the vale
Of death, and Echo, skipping
Among the rocks, are much the same.
To idle fancy both were bred;
Alas, if only they had wed!

Fragment d'une élégie

Ciel ! plane au-dessus des saisons.

De notre posthume maison,
Ardoises que souille la neige,
Vous dites assez si les anges
Ont fait leur nid près de ce toit.

Je n'y veux, ange au cœur de neige,
Nulle autre vestale que toi.

Orgues, figues, de Barbarie.

Ève sans nourrice allaitée.

Le nom de Jeanne ou de Marie.

Cimes de vertige, se rient
Des pourpres ardeurs de l'été
Vos durables virginités.

La peur de mourir, mon beau cygne,
À ton chant ôte sa beauté.

En feignant de cacher sa tête,
L'ange avec son bras souligne.

Au sein de l'amazone, tète
Ce même lait de paradis,
Qui donna la force jadis
De dire sans regret adieu
Au serpent vert, aux vertes pommes.

Fragment of an Elegy

Ye gods! To soar above the seasons...

Our posthumous dwelling
– Slates soiled with snow –
Will be commodious so long as
Angels are nesting near its roof.

Angel whose heart is pure snow,
You're the one virgin I long to know.

Barrel organs, figs of Barbary.

Eve suckled without a wet nurse.

A name like Joan or Mary.

Dizzy heights, your timeless virginity
Mocks the summer's purple swoon.

My lovely swan, the fear of dying
Robs your song of its beauty.

The angel, pretending to mask its head
With its wing, only heightens it.

At the Amazon's breast, come lap
The milk of paradise, that same milk
Which long ago gave a lover strength
To say goodbye without regret
To the lithe serpent, the unripe apples.

Prenant pour les éclairs de Dieu
La fausse lumière des hommes,
Comment pourrait se méfier,
L'ange de notre magnésium ?
Le voilà photographié.
. . . .

Taking the artificial light of man
For God's own thunderbolts,
How could the angel ever suspect
The glare of our magnesium flash?
There! – We've got its picture.

. . . .

Un cygne mort

Un cygne mort ne se remarque
Parmi l'écume au bord du lac.

Léda te voilà bien vengée,
Pense qu'un cygne au tien pareil
D'une aïeule charmant l'oreille
Au premier chant fut égorgé.

Son duvet emplit l'édredon
Sous lequel Léda délaissée
Informe de son abandon
Le passant qui déjà le sait.

Passez, couleurs, puisque tout passe,
À la fin il reste du blanc.
Les anges en peignoir de bain
Sur le sable n'ont laissé trace

De leur passage. Et les dérange
Du chien la nuit quelque aboiement ;
Le simple coup de pied d'un ange
Enseigne au chien comme l'on ment.

Et toi, mon cygne, ma tristesse,
Qu'en attendant Noël j'engraisse,
Les larmes dont ton cœur est plein
Empêchent le sang de tacher
Le sable sur lequel Léda
Pour un cygne se suicida.

Son linge, ses larmes séchés,
L'ange s'élance du tremplin.

A Lifeless Swan

A lifeless swan can't make out its image
Amid the foam by the lake's edge.

Leda, now you're quite avenged,
To think that a swan as handsome as yours,
While charming an ancestral ear with its
First fair song, was cruelly slain.

Its down is stuffing for the quilt
Beneath which ravished Leda, with her
Wild-eyed look, tells passers-by
What they already can surmise.

Fade, bright tints, since all must fade;
In the end remains only white.
Angels in their beach wraps
Have left behind in the sand

No trace of their visit. The baying
Of dogs at night annoys them;
But the merest brush of an angel's wing
Will teach a dog to hold his peace.

And you, my swan, my sorrow,
Whom I'm fattening up for Christmas,
The tears which fill your heart expunge
The bloodstains from the beach
Where Leda, all for a swan, took her life.

Its tears and beach wrap grown quite dry,
The angel springboards into the sky.

Index

Index of First Lines

ENGLISH

ALMA CLASSICS

ALMA CLASSICS aims to publish mainstream and lesser-known European classics in an innovative and striking way, while employing the highest editorial and production standards. By way of a unique approach the range offers much more, both visually and textually, than readers have come to expect from contemporary classics publishing.

To order any of our titles and for up-to-date information about our current and forthcoming publications, please visit our website on:

www.almaclassics.com

Made in United States
Orlando, FL
22 March 2026

79568208R00067